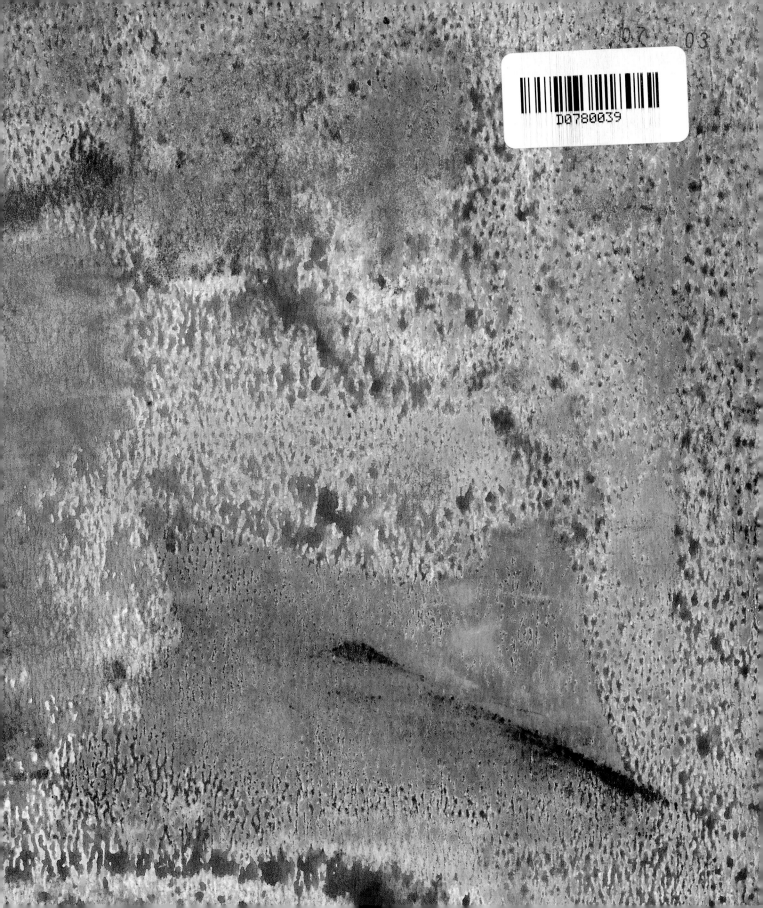

To the Plains Indians of North America,

whose everlasting art and wisdom opened the way

Book design by Patrice Sheridan

Brodsky, Beverly.
Buffalo / written and illustrated by Beverly Brodsky.-- 1st ed.
p. cm.
Summary: Presents paintings and tribal song-poems that express the
buffalo's essential and sacred role on the Plains.
ISBN 0-7614-5133-1
1. Indians of North America--Great Plains--Juvenile literature. 2.
American bison--Juvenile literature. [1. Indians of North America--Great
Plains. 2. Bison.] I. Title.
E78.G73 B684 2003      599.64'3'0978--dc21      2002009639

Printed in Malaysia
First edition
1   3   5   6   4   2

My thanks to Dr. Brian Swann for his scholarly insights and valuable instruction. Dr. Swann is Professor of English at the Cooper Union and editor of a number of volumes related to Native American literature, including, with Arnold Krupat, *Smoothing the Ground* and *Here First: Autobiographical Essays by Native American Writers*; *Recovering the Word*; *Wearing the Morning Star: Native American Song-Poems*; and *Coming to Light: Contemporary Translations of the Native Literatures of North America*. In addition, I'd like to thank the helpful librarians at the Museum of the American Indian, George Gustav Heye Center, Smithsonian Institution. Finally, I'd like to express my gratitude to George Nicholson, who encouraged me and believed in this book; to my editor, Margery Cuyler, whose special guidance helped to shape this creation; to friends and family for their support; and especially to my mother for her undying faith in me.

# BEVERLY BRODSKY

# Buffalo

*with selections from Native American Song-Poems*

*illustrated with original paintings*

Marshall Cavendish

New York

"Warrior," watercolor

*The great Father of Life*
*who made us*
*and gave us this land*
*to live upon*
*made the buffalo. . .*
*to afford us sustenance.*

—Warrior of the
northern Plains

Early images of the European wisent, a cousin of the American buffalo, appeared about twenty thousand years ago on cave walls in Altamira, Spain, and in the cave of Lascaux near Montignac, France. Scientists called this time in history the Paleolithic period.

The first artists were often nomadic hunters. They followed the animals they hunted from place to place. They speared the wisent for its flesh and hide. We think they painted images on the cave walls to summon the animal's spirit. Perhaps they thought the image was powerful enough to cause the animal to appear in the flesh.

To make color, early cave painters mixed minerals from the earth with fat, saliva, or blood. They used charcoal for making black pigment. With red, yellow, and black, they drew pictures of the wisent on cave walls. Instead of brushes they painted with twigs, reeds, feathers, fur, or the wisent's porous hump bones.

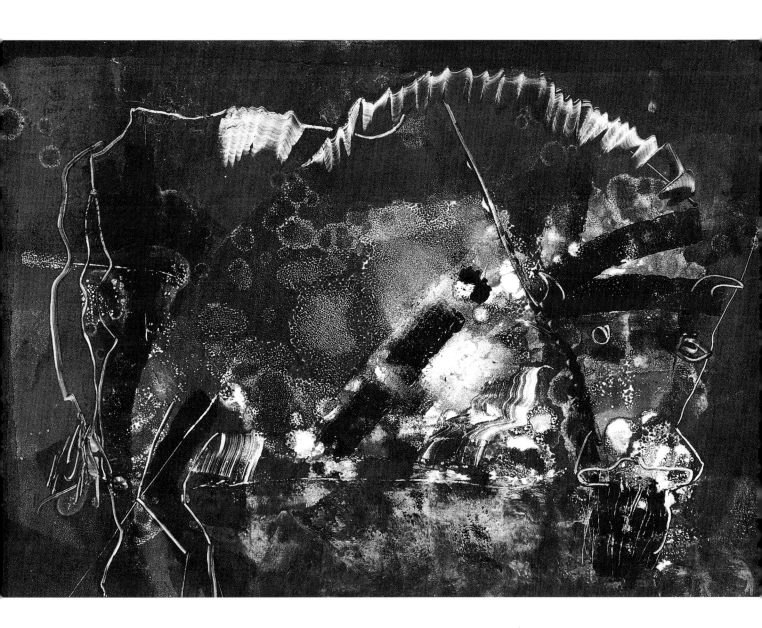

"Paleolithic Wisent," monoprint

Like the Paleolithic hunters, the first people in the United States felt a connection to the buffalo's spirit. Native Americans settled on the Plains about 4,000 years ago, long before Europeans arrived in the 1500s. The buffalo became a way of life for them. It provided food, fuel, and clothing, taking care of all their basic needs. The first Americans celebrated the buffalo's sacred spirit with ceremonies, prayers, and songs. The buffalo taught that all living things, including humans, are equal in the natural world. The Indians thought of the buffalo as their brother.

*Unreal the buffalo is standing.*
*He said, "Unreal the buffalo is standing."*
*These are his sayings:*
*"Unreal the buffalo is standing,*
*Unreal the buffalo is standing,*
*Unreal he stands in the open space,*
*Unreal he is standing."*

—excerpt from a Chahiksichahiks (Pawnee) song,
recorded by Wicita Blain

*Wicita Blain, a blind singer, led this song during a ceremonial dance after a buffalo appeared to him in a dream. The animal told him that he would live to an old age and would have the power to predict the future. Buffalo dances were performed to honor the spirit of the buffalo and often took place before a hunt. In this song "unreal" means unordinary or holy.*

"Buffalo Standing," watercolor

Every tribe had at least one shaman, or spiritual guide, who communicated with the spirit world. Before a buffalo hunt, he went into a trance to bring on a vision. In this dream state, he could see where the buffalo herds were gathered. By chanting and performing rituals, the shaman brought the buffalo to where the hunters could spear them. In some tribes, such as the Mandan, both men and women had separate hunting ceremonies. They danced through the night to summon the buffalo. Like the shaman, these "medicine hunters" called forth the buffalo spirit.

*Sun's boat is a bowl of buffalo skin,*
*a Bull-Hide canoe. His songs are the paddles.*

*At daybreak he stands in the door of his lodge*
*At the edge of the world where the earth and sky meet.*

*He paints himself red and puts on a blanket of wolf-skin,*
*A feathered, rabbit-skin headdress.*
*He lights his pipe, points it to the sky.*

*He sings, and his canoe comes down like a cloud,*
*and carries him up across the sky.*

—Mandan song recited by a Modoc medicine hunter
visiting from the south

*This song was sung during the Okippe ceremony. On the first day, a warrior painted his face red and appeared in a wolf skin, a headdress of raven feathers, and a buffalo cow's tail. Then he took a large medicine pipe and pointed it toward a canoe made of buffalo skin. "First Man" went into a trance that produced a vision of a great herd of buffalo. The next day, eight men dressed as buffalo bulls performed a dance, bellowing and roaring like buffalo while surrounding the boat.*

"Medicine Man," oil painting

The Indians of the Plains believed the Great Creator made the buffalo plentiful. There were countless millions roaming across the prairies as far as the eye could see. In the late summer and fall, carefully chosen tribal members hunted the buffalo in time to store meat for the harsh, cold winter months.

*Clouds of dust arise, rolling up from earth,*
*Spreading onward; Herds are there.*
*Speeding on before,*
*Going straight where we must journey.*

*What are those we see moving in the dust?*
*This way coming from the herd;*
*Buffalo and calf!*
*Food they promise for the children.*

—excerpt from a Chahiksichahiks (Pawnee) song sung by Tahirassuwichi, a native keeper of sacred rites, during a Hako ceremony in praise of children and peace among the tribes

*This song was sung in memory of the great herds of buffalo and the days of freedom before the Europeans came to North America. The medicine men sang the words inside the lodge during the ceremony. It was called the "Song of the Promise of the Buffalo."*

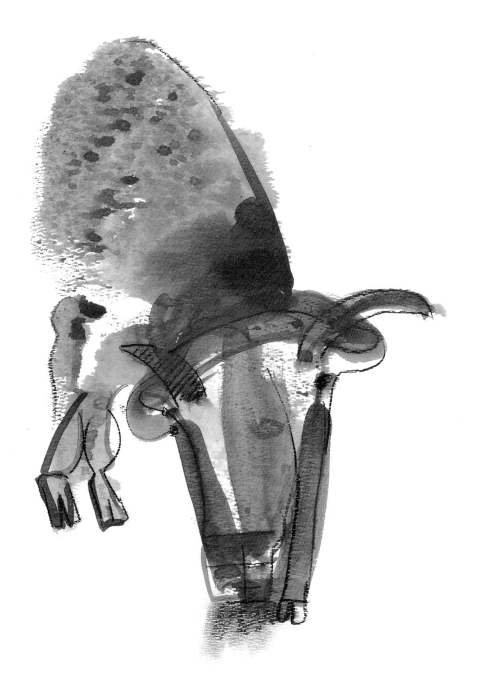

"Buffalo Drinking," watercolor and charcoal

15

"Countless Millions," watercolor

The Indians hunted the buffalo in many different ways. Before they had horses, they hunted on foot with only a lance for a weapon. As they slowly crept up to the beast, they knew that this great, shaggy animal suddenly might turn on them and gore them to death with its horns. The Native Americans also hunted with bows and arrows. Sometimes they disguised themselves in wolf skins to fool the buffalo. The hunter would creep up to the animal and, with a carefully aimed arrow, shoot the mighty creature.

*I rise, I rise,*

*I, whose tread makes the earth rumble.*

*I rise, I rise,*

*I, in whose thighs there is strength.*

*I rise, I rise,*

*I, who whips his back with his tail when in rage.*

*I rise, I rise,*

*I, who shakes his mane when angered.*

*I rise, I rise,*

*I, in whose humped shoulders there is power.*

*I rise, I rise,*

*I, whose horns are sharp and curved.*

—"Rising of Buffalo Bull Men, song #1,"
Wazhazhe (Osage) song, sung by Waxthi'zhi

*In this song the buffalo is called upon for its spiritual power. The words describe a buffalo's anger.*

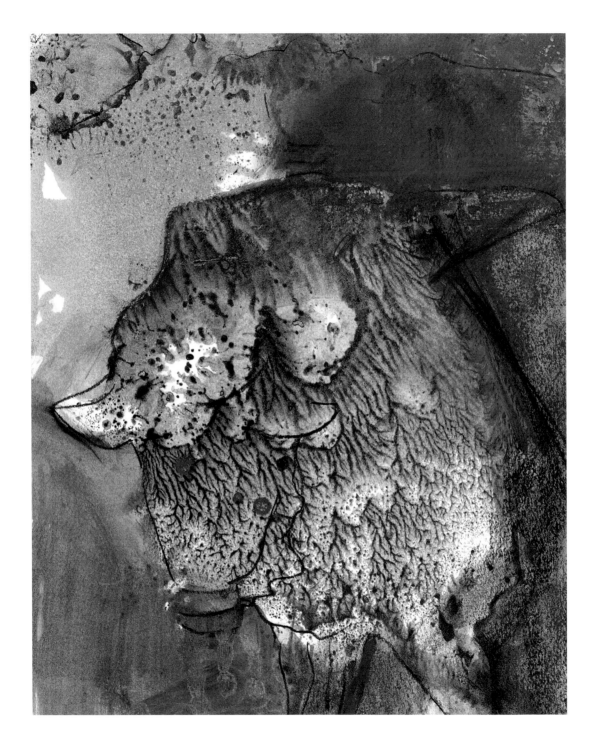

"Speared Buffalo," oil and charcoal

After the Spanish brought horses to North America in the 1500s, the medicine hunters became skilled horsemen. While riding bareback, they used bows and arrows to kill the buffalo.

Sometimes the hunters herded the buffalo into a tight circle. The animal became an easy target as the men closed in on it.

The first Americans also created buffalo stampedes, driving a herd of buffalo over the high cliffs, where the animals fell to their death in the gorge below. The stampedes left more buffalo dead than were needed for survival.

*He! They have come back racing.*
*Why, they say there is to be*
*a Buffalo Hunt over here,*
*Make arrows! Make arrows!*
*says the Father, says the Father.*

—Sioux song

*A scouting party on a journey to find the buffalo might have sung this song as they raced back to camp. Perhaps a shaman also sang this song during a New Moon ceremony. The lines explain that the Creator, or Great Spirit, wants arrows to be made. The Sioux formed arrows from the buffalo's hind leg. They dried the heavy sinews and cut them up into arrow points.*

"The Hunt," watercolor

After the hunt the shaman gave thanks and offered a dead buffalo as a gift to the Great Spirit. The women skinned the hides and butchered the meat. With their flint knives they cut up the flesh. The medicine hunters ate the first pieces of meat. Then the meat was divided and shared by all. Around a big fire, everyone celebrated the hunt by feasting, singing songs, and honoring the buffalo with prayers and dances. All through the night, storytellers spun traditional tales about their brother the buffalo, their ancestors' heroic deeds, and the Great Spirit. Children listened to these oral legends in the warmth of the fire. They knew these teachings were sacred and must be remembered and retold.

*"Give me my knife*
*I shall hang meat to dry"—Ye'ye!*
*Says the grandmother—Yo'yo!*
*"When it is dry,*
*I shall make pemmican!"*
*Says the grandmother—Yo'yo!*

—Dakota Song

*This song is about making pemmican, a mixture of dried buffalo meat, mashed berries, and fat. It was made by women at the end of a buffalo hunt and stored in hides. The grandmother in the song represents Mother Earth in human form. The pemmican helped the Dakota survive the hard winters.*

"Dead Buffalo," watercolor and oil

No part of the buffalo was wasted. The women made shoes, clothes, and tepees from the hide. The tongue and bone marrow, as well as the meat, provided nutrition. The animal's horns and bones were sharpened into tools and used as part of ceremonial masks. The tendons, bones, and sinews were made into weapons. Even the bladder was not wasted but was shaped into a water carrier.

*I want the robes, the skins*
*of the game animals. Bring*
*them to me. Let us enjoy*
*ourselves.*

*Spring from the earth, food*
*for our children. Give us*
*good health. Let us grow up*
*and become ripe.*

—Hidatsa song from the Buffalo Dance Society

*This and other songs were sung by selected members of a sacred society. There is a legend that the leader was once a buffalo that later assumed human form and communicated with the buffalo spirit. During a full winter moon, the songs were chanted to summon the buffalo. The society members made a pipe offering to a row of buffalo hide headdresses and then to the sky, the four directions, and the earth. The Hidatsa believed that these songs would bring heavy snow, which would drive the buffalo toward the Indian hunters. "Spring from the earth, food for our children" could be a reference to the good harvest that would feed the children and provide well-being for the whole tribe.*

"Crow Parfleche Made
from Buffalo Rawhide,"
watercolor on gessoed paper

"Sioux Spoon Made
from a Buffalo Horn,"
watercolor on gessoed paper

"Sioux Buffalo Hide Tipi Cover," watercolor on gessoed paper

25

The Plains Indians had no word for *art*, but two Dakota words come close to its meaning: *Wake wayupika* (to make form, or to make skillful). The Plains tribes crafted many beautiful objects from parts of the buffalo. The Crow (Absaroke), the Cheyenne, the Gros Ventre, and the Mandan were among the tribes that painted on buffalo skins. Like the Paleolithic artists, they made colors by mixing minerals from the earth with natural ingredients. These included the insides of birds' eggs, the juice of the prickly pear, and buffalo suet.

"Mandan Buffalo Bull Boat," gouache on gessoed paper

"Apache Buffalo Horn Headdress," gouache on gessoed paper

"Cheyenne Ghost Dance Moccasins," gouache on gessoed paper

"Sioux Shield," gouache on gessoed paper

"Crow War Regalia Case," gouache on gessoed paper

"Sioux Buffalo Robe," gouache on gessoed paper

The whole world is coming.
A nation is coming, a nation is coming.
The Eagle has brought the message to the tribe.
The father says so, the father says so.

Over the whole earth they are coming.
The buffalo are coming, the buffalo are coming.
The Crow has brought the message to the tribe.
The father says so, the father says so.

It is I who made these sacred things,
Says the father, says the father.
It is I who made the sacred shirt,
Says the father, says the father.
It is I who made the pipe,
Says the father, says the father.

"The Eagle," gouache on gessoed paper

—fragment of a Sioux song used during a Ghost Dance ceremony

The Ghost Dance came to Wovoka, a Paiute prophet, in the form of a vision. The dance became part of a movement in the 1880s to preserve Native American Plains culture from changes brought by the white man. Ghost Dance ceremonies celebrated the peace the Indians enjoyed before the Europeans invaded their land. Their rituals expressed the hope that all people would live again in peace. The movement ended in 1890, when U.S. soldiers attacked and killed about 250 worshipers at Wounded Knee, North Dakota. The song above was repeated during a dance describing the coming of the Great Change—the return of the buffalo and the spirits of the departed. The message was brought to the people by the sacred birds, the eagle and the crow. The last six lines refer to the sacred pipe and the Ghost Shirt worn during the ceremony.

By the end of the nineteenth century, the buffalo had all but vanished. From the 1830s to the 1860s, European settlers killed the animals for greed and sport. Skulls, bones, and carcasses dotted the Great Plains. Gathered, stacked, and transported by railcars journeying to the east, the dead animals were turned into trophies, glue, fertilizer, and furniture. The buffalo could no longer provide Native Americans with the means to survive. The animals were hunted to near extinction.

Along with the buffalo, thousands of Plains Indians perished. Those who survived were forced onto reservations and Army camps, often far away from their own land. Instead of painting on buffalo hides, the Indians began to chronicle events in ledgers on paper.

"Buffalo Skulls," gouache and watercolor

*Listen,*
*the song of the*
*aged father.*

*The song of the*
*aged beloved,*
*our father*
*the buffalo*
*heavy with age,*
*endlessly walking,*

*too heavy to*
*rise again*
*if he should fall.*

*Walking forever,*
*walking forever,*
*humped high with age,*
*head bent with age.*

*Heavy with age,*
*heavy with age.*

*Aged buffalo,*
*my aged father.*

—Chahiksichahiks (Pawnee)
Buffalo Dance song, recorded
by Wicita Blain

"Heavy with Age," watercolor and ink

*This song was sung during a solemn ceremonial dance held in a large earthen lodge. It describes how a very old buffalo repeatedly falls down after struggling to rise to his feet. He is simply too old and too heavy to get up.*

In 1830 there were about 60 million buffalo roaming the Plains. By 1893 there were less than 500. Since then there have been efforts to increase the number of buffalo in the United States. On December 8, 1905, the American Bison Society was formed and began to stock a number of wildlife preserves. By 1930 the number of buffalo had grown to about 4,000. Satisfied with the number, the society stopped its activities. Ranchers and breeders later formed the National Bison Association. Today there are about 150,000 buffalo in private and public herds. These strong beasts, once again living in national parks and on reservations (Cheyenne, Sioux, Chippewa, and Osage) and grazing on prairie land, keep alive the ancient spirit of the buffalo. The poems and songs of Native Americans ensure that the spirit of the buffalo will live on into eternity.

*Clear the way,*
*In a sacred manner I come.*
*The earth is mine,*
*Hence in a sacred manner I come.*
*Clear the way,*
*In a sacred manner I come.*

—Bear Eagle, contemporary Teton Sioux Lakota

*This poem speaks of the renewal of the earth and can also be interpreted as the return of a rich culture from the past.*

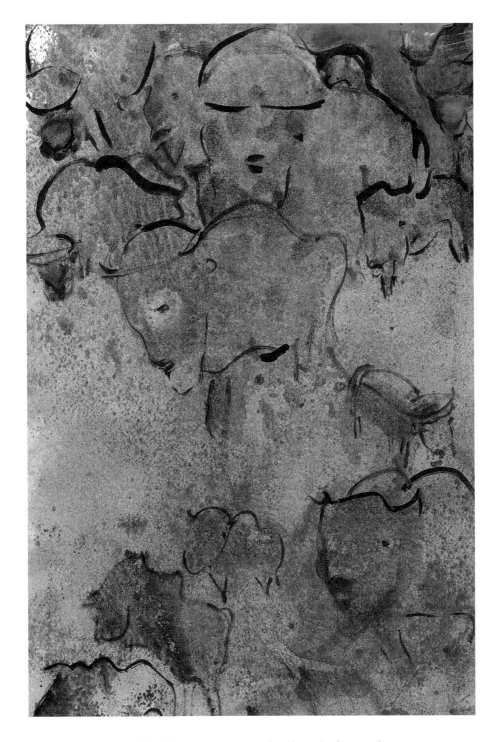

"Buffalo Returning," oil and charcoal

# A Note from the Author

This book developed from a number of influences. No doubt its roots lie in my early visits to the American Museum of Natural History and the Brooklyn Museum in New York City, where I gazed at ancient paintings of buffalo by Shoshone, Sioux, and Cheyenne artists. Their pictographs recorded the hunt, buffalo migrations, and tribal wars. As I grew older, I read Olaf Baker's romantic legend, "Where the Buffaloes Begin." Recently I studied the European wisent in reproductions of ancient cave paintings from Altamira, Spain, and from the cave of Lascaux in France. Also, among the spiritual teachings of John (Fire) Lame Deer (contemporary Lakota Sioux), I discovered the quote, "The buffalo is our Brother almost like a part of ourselves, part of our souls." Unfortunately, over time, much of the picture writing on buffalo hides has all but disappeared, along with other traditional objects that were an integral part of Native American culture. Sadly, when the Indian population declined along with the buffalo and whole tribes were wiped out, the remaining few were forced into military camps and onto reservations. During that time, many of the sacred objects were either lost or destroyed. I am grateful, therefore, for all the material I was able to find in museums and library collections, particularly the ledgers on paper that the Indian historians kept for the community at the end of the nineteenth century. Some of these ledgers were drawn by powerful chiefs or appointed chroniclers. Among them were Eaglelance (Amos Bad Heart Buffalo) and Nupa Kte (Kills Two) of the Oglala Sioux, as well as Chief Washake of the Shoshone (Nimic) tribe. He said, "A people without a history is like the wind on the buffalo grass." In addition to original Indian paintings, I've discovered the nineteenth-century European painters who visited various tribes, recorded scenes of daily life, and painted portraits of the great chiefs and medicine men. These painters include George Catlin, Karl Bodmer, and Alfred Jacob Miller.

Like Catlin, Bodmer, Miller, and others, artists throughout time have painted images for different reasons. Often these images are only symbolic extensions of thoughts, dreams and desires; but they also can be an attempt to reach the light and dark of one's soul, one's inner being. In the process of creation, some twentieth-century artists have drawn upon the past in order to express what moves them in the present. Pablo Picasso, Paul Klee, Jackson Pollock, and Mark Rothko all absorbed either African or Indian elements into their own work. Many of these timeless images have been integral to their paintings, although there is a fresh and unique vision that is born from these inheritances. I too feel my paintings have gained strength from the images of the past, deepening my understanding and spirituality as I move into the future.

"Buffalo on the Prairie," watercolor

33

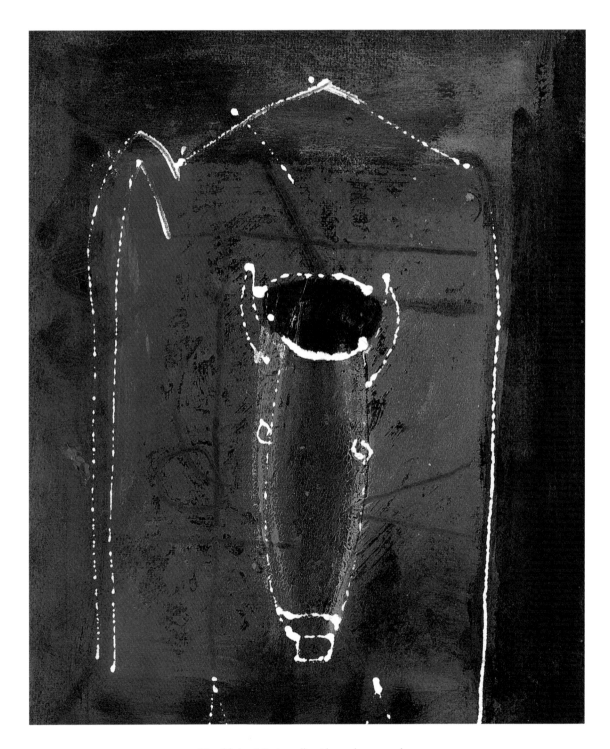

"Buffalo Vision," oil and gouache

# Buffalo

*My imagination comes,*

*An arrow in the night.*

*In the mist a dream comes.*

*The bull leaves only bones,*

*His horns rattle in the night.*

*Death comes with the arrow*

*In the night.*

*The arrow pierces the brow of heaven.*

*It shrieks in the night—*

*In the sky.*

*The bull leaves his bones for the night.*

*He lays down*

*In the night.*

*His hooves grip the sky.*

*His soul stampedes toward heaven.*

*His breath becomes another life.*

—Beverly Brodsky

# Sources for the song-poems in this book

Page 12, "Unreal the buffalo is standing"
from Fletcher, Alice C., "The Hako: A Pawnee Ceremony." Bureau of Ethnology. *Twenty-second Annual Report of the Bureau of Ethnology*. Washington, D.C., 1904. Information on the song-poem from Soens, A. L. *I, the Song, Classical Poetry of Native North America*. Salt Lake City: University of Utah Press, 1999.

Page 14, "Sun's boat is a bowl of buffalo skin"
from "Modoc Song." Translated by Alfred L. Kroeber. Bureau of American Ethnology. *Handbook of California Indians*, Bulletin # 78. Washington, D.C., 1925. Information on the song-poem from *People of the First Man, Life Among the Plains Indians in Their Final Days of Glory, The Firsthand Account of Prince Maximilian's Expedition up the Missouri River, 1833–34*. Edited and designed by Davis Thomas and Karen Ronnefeldt. New York: E.P. Dutton & Co., Inc., 1976.

Pages 16–17, "Clouds of dust arise, rolling up from earth"
from Fletcher, Alice C., "The Hako: A Pawnee Ceremony." Bureau of Ethnology. *Twenty-second Annual Report of the Bureau of Ethnology*. Washington, D.C., 1904. Information on the song-poem from Soens, A. L. *I, the Song, Classical Poetry of Native North America*. Salt Lake City: University of Utah Press, 1999.

Page 20, "I rise, I rise"
from La Flesche, Francis, "Song of the Buffalo Bull gens, Tho-xe pa the-hon," "The Osage Tribe." Bureau of American Ethnology. *Rite of Chiefs: Sayings of the Ancient Men, Thirty-sixth Annual Report of the Bureau of American Ethnology*. Washington, D.C., 1921. Information on the song-poem from Soens, A. L. *I, the Song, Classical Poetry of Native North America*. Salt Lake City: University of Utah Press, 1999.

Page 22, "He! They have come back racing"
Song-poem and information on it from Mooney, James, "The Ghost-Dance Religion and the Sioux Outbreak of 1890," Bureau of Ethnology. *Fourteenth Annual Report of the Bureau of Ethnology*. Washington, D.C., 1896.

Page 24, "Give me my knife"
Song-poem and information on it from Soens, A. L. *I, the Song, Classical Poetry of Native North America*. Salt Lake City: University of Utah Press, 1999.

Page 24, "The buffalo are coming"
from *The Indian Journals 1859–62*. Edited by Henry Lewis Morgan. Ann Arbor: University of Michigan Press, 1959. Information on the song-poem from Densmore, Frances, "Mandan and Hidatsa Music, 1867–1957," Bureau of American Ethnology. Bulletin #80. Washington, D.C., 1923.

Page 26, "I want the robes, the skins"
From *The Indian Journals 1859–62*. Edited by Henry Lewis Morgan. Ann Arbor: University of Michigan Press, 1959. Information on the song-poem from Soens, A. L. *I, the Song, Classical Poetry of Native North America*. Salt Lake City: University of Utah Press, 1999.

Page 28, "The whole world is coming"
Song-poem and information in it from Mooney, James, "The Ghost-Dance Religion and the Sioux Outbreak of 1890." Bureau of Ethnology. *Fourteenth Annual Report of the Bureau of Ethnology*. Washington, D.C., 1896.

Page 31, "Listen"
Song-poem adaptation and information on it from a translation by Densmore, Frances, "Pawnee Music." Bureau of American Ethnology, Bulletin #93. Washington, D.C., 1929.

Page 34, "Clear the Way." Copyright © 1997 by Diane Hoyt-Goldsmith. Reprinted from *"Buffalo Days"* by permission of Holiday House, Inc.

# Index

Page numbers in *italics* are illustrations.

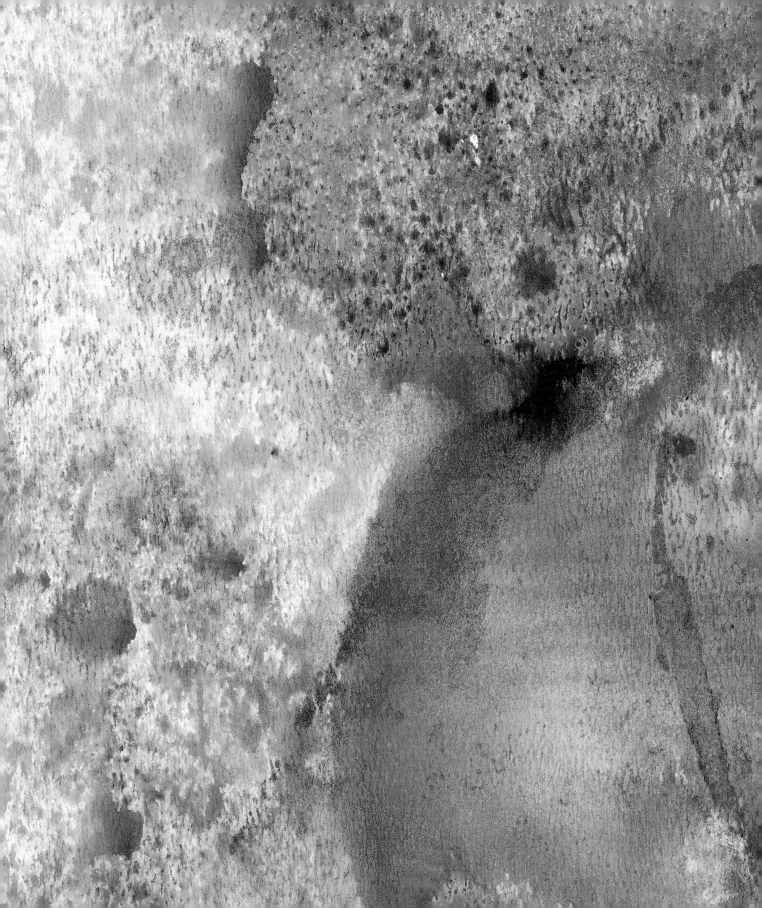